Prologue: Introducing Sherlock Bond and why I am sharing these debriefs from previous missions with VILLAINS!

First off, I want to say a huge thank you for taking the time read my story. My name is Greg Holroyd the so-called Sherlock Bond of these stories…

I decided to write these stories as a big part of my journey in life was derailed a little particularly after graduating from the secret spy academy (university). You see I had only gone to university because it was shoved down my throat at school it was the best option but more importantly to make momma magic proud which I'm sure she was.

The problem was once I had achieved this goal I was a little lost and in limbo… I ended up flying out to America to teach magic at a summer camp which I went back to for two seasons and is where I found my passion as a coach/mentor! Some of the best memories I have in my life to this date and still catch myself thinking about the ILC crew from 2014-2015.

It was during my time away from summer camp my life was a little bit of a circus as you'll see in the following pages due to my own decisions to surround myself with toxic people, narcissists, psychopaths and what I like to call in my online courses, VILLAINS!

I've been asked by other people and even myself WHY I am sharing these stories… Some saying I am holding on to the emotions to the stories which at various stages in my life this may have been the case. Yes, I am trying to share the pain I was experiencing during these moments but between the lines are important lessons to take away to help repel these creatures who sadly walk among us… I have moved on from all these situations, in a much better place in life and have forgiven all of these villains for my own well-being. A big lesson I hope you take away from this book.

If you don't know anything about my professional background I have two business's or ways of making money if you will. I'm a magician, mind-reader, hypnotist and gentlemen pickpocket hired to entertain at weddings & events providing unforgettable entertainment with magic memories! If you happen to know any new engaged couples or big events coming up please do feel free to share my magic wanky website at: www.gregholroyd.co.uk

I also speak and coach about reading & influencing human behaviour to connect with the right people, build trust during discovering more win-win opportunities in our personal/ business relationships and getting people to persuades themselves within negotiation! Or simply I help you read people like Sherlock Holmes with the social skills of James Bond! I will leave links for the online academy throughout the book and you can find out more

about my speaking & coaching services at
www.magicspeaker.co.uk

Anyway now we got the promo BS out of
the way I wanted to say if any of these stories
resonates with you as the reader, I've included
both personal and professional situations in
these stories please talk to someone you trust
ASAP. I promise it will help you and I may
have something that may help you as I offer a
FREE mini course to help repel the villains and
have left a link below so you can get access
with just an email address.
www.magicspeaker.gurucan.com

With that being said if you can't tell I
love Batman, Sherlock Holmes and James
Bond! So in attempt to keep every one
anonymous I'll be using fun little word plays to
keep these stories that way, as well as being
hilarious at times.

I was scared to release this book as I
made a lot of mistakes along the way and do
not consider myself a hero in these stories,
rather a vigilante spy constantly learning. I
hope you find these stories funny due to the
way I have written them and highlighted the

lessons between the lines. I wanted to share my own experiences to put a smile on peoples face whilst educating, one of my life missions! There are lessons within every series of manipulation I hope will help you repel VILLAINS within your own life & the courage to get help if you need an EXIT!

So now you know why these stories are so important to me and why I'm sharing them. Let's start these stories the way I have always wanted to by saying again from the bottom of my heart thank you for reading what's in these pages. My names is Greg Holroyd or for the purposes of these stories, it's Bond…Sherlock Bond…

(cue awesome music)

Sherlock Bond has Cothams Tiddler as his landlord who tries to bully him & how Sherlock outsmarted him to escape!

Chaper 1: Sherlock meets Cothams Tiddler and living around lots of bad apples…

Sherlock had got a bus to meet Tiddler for the first time in a block of flats in an area he didn't know for viewing in Cotham. Tiddler came across as a nice guy during viewing, easy to get along with and Sherlock didn't suspect a thing (Just like any villain). The place was really small but Sherlock needed to get out of his Dad's place who had been kind enough to put him up for a few months and had overstayed his welcome.... So Sherlock had gone online to do his intel spy thing (googled local flats & house shares in the area) and that is how he found & met the Tiddler. Sherlock paid 3 months up front & moved in… He did think at the time it was a little strange Tiddler didn't ask for his I.D. and the paperwork was a little off compared to his previous tenancies but he needed to find a place ASAP and was close enough to city centre for him perform and network for his business.

So he moved in and only really connected with one person at the start known as the Whiney Penguin (a character in another story). Compared to everyone else in the flats who were addicts, crooks and bad apples in general Whiney Penguin was OK at this point... Occasionally you would get normal people who would use the block for 2-3 months and quickly move on (Sherlock now understands why).

Whiney Penguin seemed the most normal as you will understand as the story unfolds... He was maybe 3-4 years younger than

Sherlock, a bartender & both were down on their luck trying to get back their our feet. It is worth noting Sherlock didn't have any friends in the area at the time and Whiney Penguin was one of the few people he would hang out with outside of working on his business…

The first 3-4 months were kind of ok… The other tenants were a little crazy at weekends but Sherlock was performing & picking pockets whilst busking in the bars of Cotham so much he didn't really notice how bad things were going to get… He also didn't realise he was being massively overcharged for a shoebox of a flat with an oven he couldn't use because it produce outrageous amount of smoke signals and lived off fried food, microwave meals & takeouts during this time. Due to just getting back on his feet during his sofa surfing days this is how Sherlock got by. He was in a weird place in his life where he was a little clueless, only just graduating from spy college (university) and pretending to run a business rather than actually running a business…

Chapter 2: Living in the slums of Cotham &
Sherlock starts finally seeing the neighbours for
what they are…

Sherlock slowly started noticing what
was really going on with one of the tenants we
will call Red… She can only be politely
described as an escort who had a drug problem
with red hair. She also had a brother who
wasn't actually her brother between them they
would cause all kinds of havoc in the block.

They were vile creatures Sherlock would
often overhear scheming with each other
through the window of his flat how they were
going mug vulnerable people in the area &
were well known for it! Sherlock started
coming home to all kinds of nonsense, random
people in the yard, the rancid smell of crack
being smoked in the flat below, weird animal
noises from the flat below and the police were
knocking on Sherlocks & neighbours doors
asking for people all the time (Usually Red &
her "brother"). Things were starting to affect

Sherlocks mental health looking back, his insomnia was really out of control during this time and Sherlock was easily talked into post-busking drinks and smoking cannabis back then.

There was a bunch of other minor villains who were living here, not as bad as a Red & her brother, but still didn't make life easy for Sherlock... Red would also bring her friends/ customers to the block of flats and Sherlock would have to regularly walk past her front door where a horrible horrendous chemical smell would be especially during the weekend evenings... At the start Sherlock could tolerate Red, he would say hello if he passed her and give her papers for cigarettes if she asked... keep the peace and all that.

That all changed one night when she was out of her face on god knows what and decided to pick a fight with Sherlock on his way home from the shops. Having no idea why, Sherlock put the key code into the gate to get into the block garden that took him to his front door & that's when she came up behind him shouting at Sherlock! Threatening him with all kinds of craziness, how he needed to be careful & watch himself. He had no idea what was going on and tried talking her down but when he saw her brother & another figure he made the decision to get in his own flat ASAP and make a call to the Tiddler and leave him a text message, always leave written proof of communication for complaints, especially with suspected villains as landlords & in the workplace...

After an evening in Sherlocks own flat where he didn't get the best night sleep, Tiddler had responded to his message and said he was on his way to deal with Red. He came over that day had a chat with Red who later gave a forced apology to Sherlock and it wouldn't happen again (it did!). Before Tiddler left the blocks he came to visit Sherlock at his flat to explain that he had a chat to Red, PROMISED the madness would never happen again and if it did there would be consequences for Red...

This is only 1 out of the 2 times Sherlock saw Tiddler for a complaints, as Tiddler would only ever come out to speak to tenants, usually

Red, for serious incidences (this and the time one of Reds friends smashed her window and break into her flat). Tiddler would leave the smaller incidents to the on site manager Blue Bird who we will introduce in the next chapter!

Chapter 3: Sherlock is under Tiddlers control without knowing and meeting Blue-Bird

Sherlock started making complaints to the on site manager, Blue-Bird. Blue-Bird was a big tall older man, with a bigger belly and a moustache that Sherlock would see every week to pay his rent. Blue-Bird had his own ground floor flat and covered in tattoos of his local football team. He would often be found stood at his front door with nothing but a pair of boxers on, working hard with a cigarette in his mouth, leaning on the door frame and if you ever needed to knock on his door for something, this is how he would answer… Sherlock is still working out to this day if this was his work uniform.

Sherlock didn't actually have a problem with Blue-Bird, he was easy enough to get along with and just lazy… Sherlock eventually got annoyed how Blue-Bird pretty much ignored all his complaints about Red & her brother and said unless they are caught the act there's nothing he could do… Despite Sherlock and everyone else knowing what exactly was going on, they were living on top of each other FFS!!! The thing was Red and Big-Bird were really good friends and Sherlock would often hear Red squawk his name through his letter box early hours of the morning asking to borrow money. Looking back Sherlock should've known this place was dump to be in and should have got out a lot sooner. But he did what a lot of us do as human beings...He talked himself into a bad situation! Sherlock Bond says this all the time, we talk ourselves OUT of GOOD situations and IN to BAD ones!

Sherlock came home from work one evening and was attacked on the stairs outside leading to the front yard to get to his front door and was forced into a position where unfortunately he had to defend myself against a knife. That night was was incredibly stressful and he can still remember to this day the amount of adrenaline going through his body hours after the event… That being said, he is proud of how he managed the situation, maintaining distance, talking the person down to buy time and despite ripping one of his favourite backpacks. He was able to make sure the sharp/pointy object stayed away from his body and he is still alive today to tell the story.

The other thing we are going to quickly mention here is Sherlock had met, BatBoy. BatBoy was another person Sherlock met in the flats and had moved in above him about 6 months into his tenancy. Sherlock had helped BatBoy as he was also being messed around by Tiddler and this is probably the reason why they Sherlock & BatBoy bonded dealing with so much of Tiddlers BS. Little did Sherlock know at the time BatBoy was also a villain he would tell you about in a much funnier story.

Tiddler had somehow charged BatBoy extra for rent, something to do with a claim BatBoy had and that he hadn't received rent... There was always something off about Tiddlers reasoning and would later find out he had all kinds of side deals for money with tenants. These should have been huge red flags but Sherlock was blind at the time with minimal spy training. At least 4 other tenants he knew were having problems and being charged extra for rent one or another by Tiddler, vulnerable people who were probably confused to what was happening.

Because Sherlock was paying mainly cash straight to Big-Bird, using his tip money from busking and topping up with bank withdrawals. Sherlock never had to do anything like this with Tiddler but tried to help BatBoy anyway he could. Sherlock ended up helping BatBoy out of this situation & ended bringing BatBoy into his new house share, HUGE MISTAKE!

One of the things Sherlock started to notice with most of the other tenants in these flats is they all seemed to have their own personal problems, be it addiction, housing, separation, immigrants and just people who were vulnerable one way or another… It was almost like the landlord was targeting these kind of people who were struggling in life with addiction, not knowing laws of a new country, mental health problems and more. It wasn't until after Sherlock had moved out that he really clocked this and makes him wonder just how many of the tenants were victims of Tiddlers evil plans…

These days Sherlock always take note of the environment he is in, what is happening around him and who is around him etc. as it can be easy becoming blind to the red flags of villains even when the signs are right in front of you.

Chapter 4: Reds friend breaks into her flat, Sherlock refuses to pay rent and storing bullets to use later in self defence!

It got to a point where Sherlock started to stop paying rent as Tiddler was refusing to do anything about the situation. Tiddler had only come out twice as this point, once in the previous chapter and another time when one of Reds friends had thrown a brick through her window! It was amazing how quick he came over for that complaint! But when Sherlock and other tenants had made complaints, nothing happened it seemed. Sherlock remembers him coming to see him after explaining how she would have to pay for the window which Sherlocks response was, "great but how does that help my situation? Don't get me wrong I'm glad YOUR window will be getting fixed but charging her for window does what for me? I'm still dealing with her BS?"

It was probably at this point Tiddler knew Sherlock wouldn't drop this and that his normal tactics of manipulation weren't going to work as Sherlock wasn't vulnerable like his other tenant's… Some time went by and as things didn't get better Sherlock told Tiddler he would stop paying his rent, which he did!

Tiddler wouldn't move Red out to the block of flats as he owned another block down the road but she had caused problems with tenants there (surprise). He was making excuses & didn't want to move her! However, Sherlock was expected to move to the same place, a well known dodgier block and pay MORE rent which he wasn't in a position or wanted to do. Tiddler kept promising things would calm down but they never did and ultimately Sherlock had a final meeting with him about a year to a year and a half after he had initially moved in...

After Sherlock racked up bill of over £2k over the course of about two to two and half months, it was that expensive to live in this hell hole! Sherlock was prepared to pay this bill IF the issues he was experiencing were addressed but he had a gut feeling they wouldn't after months of complaints with evidence. So Sherlock was looking at some other options just in case he needed to move elsewhere. Sherlock had told told this to Tiddler which for some reason thought he was lying. He had a meeting with Tiddler and to this day is one of the funniest meetings Sherlocks has experienced with a landlord… It is also a negotiation against a villain he is super proud of as looking back how he handled the situation. He had done so like a true spy!

It started with Tiddler saying he needed proof Red was indeed what Sherlock said she was, an escort with a drug problem... That was fine Sherlock did a quick google, "Cotham Escort", 5 minutes later he had found a profile with a big ugly picture of Red on his phone & showed the Tiddler... He watched him swallow hard, look at the ground and proceeded stuttering some new BS...

This was the moment Sherlock knew NOTHING was going to change, that he had to move out of the place ASAP and that it was highly likely his assumptions about Tiddler were true... Tiddler was indeed a DODGY LANDLORD! Sherlock found out later Tiddler was running a variety of illegal schemes with his tenants to get more money & was charging Red 2-3 times the rent of anyone else, which would make a lot of sense looking back!

Tiddler then went through some BS plan he had clearly been rehearsing calling police, asking what they could do and after about 30 minutes Sherlock said to him, "well if nothing is going to get better I'm going to sign a tenancy agreement this week with a new letting agency and I'd be moving on..." His exact words were, "well Sherlock, thing is Red has her rent paid up and your now £2k in your arrears, I don't think you've looked anywhere else. So yeah not sure what you're trying to pull here mate?"

Sherlock quickly thanked him for his time and showed him the door about 4 minute after that statement, rolled a smoke as he watched Tiddler drive off through his window. Sherlock laughing to himself waited about 6 minutes before proceeding to go for a walk down the street as he called the other letting agency giving them the heads up he would be dropping by the office in about 9 minutes to sign the tenancy agreement for the new house share he viewed the previous day.

Sherlock to this day doesn't know why Tiddler had assumed he wasn't in the position to move out or why he didn't believe Sherlock was ready to walk. Not only was Sherlock ready to walk but he was about to take all of those bullets he had been gathering for the past year or so from Tiddler and use them in a text message to ensure he would never hear from Tiddler again!

Gathering bullets is just simply learning more information about the villain and storing away ready to use at the right time. In Tiddlers case it was all of his BS messages/excuses, not giving Sherlock back his tenancy agreement which he had been asking for months, a recording of the last meeting and much more! Sherlock was packed up, locked, loaded and ready to leave the next day to his new house and read to send THE MESSAGE!

Chapter 5: The message Sherlock sent that allowed him to escape Tiddler and how the bullets fired within it kept him away!

Sherlock only owned minimal amount of material items during this time so he could easily move into the new place without anyone knowing, particularly Blue-Bird. Plus he was moving out with Batboy whose friend was providing the car to move their belongings to the new place & as BatBoy lived above Sherlock in the block they created a spy relocation system. They moved most Sherlocks stuff to the new place first. As Sherlock did this BatBoy moved all his items from his flat to Sherlocks as he lived above him. Neither of them wanted Tiddler or Blue-Bird knowing they were moving (despite warning him) until they had actually moved out just in case Tiddler decided to throw a curve ball at them.

This was perfect because it wasn't until after all Sherlocks stuff was in the new house and they were loading up the last few bits of BatBoys stuff in the car they got to see Blue-Birds face on the final load up seeing him realise Sherlock & BatBoy were bouncing from block. They never said anything to Blue-Bird but you could tell by stupid blank look on his face whilst stood in his doorway, in his boxers, Tiddler had miscalculated his evil plan and they were GONE!

About an hour after they got BatBoys stuff to new place and paid some cash to BayBoys buddy who helped them move their stuff to new place. Sherlock sent Tiddler a text message letting him know he had moved out that day and that he was withholding ALL payments as he believe he shouldn't have had to deal with the craziness he went through as a tenant. Sherlock also explained he had video, audio and pictures of everything that had happened (even a recording of their last meeting with all his bullying techniques Tidder tried), that he needed a copy of the tenancy agreement which Tiddler never gave back to him after repeatedly asking for, a break down of the rent costs and that he would be going to Citizens Advice to discuss his next actions… Tiddler responded the text message no more than 8 minutes later "No problem, don't worry about the rent." Sherlock & Batboy were FREE! They had moved out into their new house share where Sherlock had to battle (and slap!) some sense into the BatBoy later… But that is for another story.

Two of the biggest fears villains have are abandonment and being exposed for what they are to the world. When you keep bullets against them that targets at least one of these fears, depending on the person, you have all the ingredients needed to exit these situations quickly with minimal amount of fuss. Threatening to expose Tiddler, especially to the housing authorities is why Sherlock was able to move out of this hell hole into a new and much nicer place!

Some of you might be thinking that sounds like what the villains do and you would be absolutely right! The best way to deal with these kinds of individuals is to use their own tactics against them. The key difference in understanding ethics of gathering, storing and shooting bullets is the intention. The villains do this to shoot people for fun. We do so only as a means of defence and only shoot warning shots when threatened or kill shots when attacked! The last message Sherlock had sent was indeed a kill shot at the Tiddler!

Sherlock later realised just how much of a fool the landlord had taken him for and despite the fact he was slow in getting out of that horrendous place. It was because he exited in such a way whereby he could use Tiddlers rent money to pay his new landlord for the new house (which turned out to be an incredible home with some amazing people) and Sherlock would never have to deal with Tiddler or any of the tenants again (except for two which is another story).

The reason why Tiddler never got back in touch with Sherlock was he was scared of being exposed to people, particularly going to Citizens Advice & housing authorities because they both knew what Tiddler was doing was illegal and if he had a leg to stand on like any decent/legit landlord would, he would've given

Sherlock all things he asked for in that message.

Sherlocks only regrets here are not moving out sooner and the defending himself with violence however it was necessary... But he learnt from this and let's be honest, it is rare you will handle these situations perfectly. Even with the right training you always have to adapt to the circumstances in these situations which can always change at any given moment... Be adaptable to the present situation!

So that is the story of how Sherlock outsmarted the Cothams Tiddler & escaping to a new safer place.

Sherlock Bond lives with Batboy & Whiney Penguin & how he defeated his first PERSONAL villain!

Chapter 1: Backstory of villains he brought into the house share from Tiddlers nightmare and how seeing them is often not enough!

      This story is about the two villains who almost destroyed one of the best house shares Sherlock had been in and how they tried & failed miserably to ruin relationships in his life! Batboy was someone who Sherlock had met towards the end of his tenancy with the Tiddler (We've told this previous story). Sherlock knew BatBoy was a classic womaniser, seeing multiple women at once, always blaming them for his problems and coming up with crazy stories about them all the time. A single dad with 2 kids from different relationships that in the 2-3 years Sherlock knew him, he never saw or heard of him seeing the kids. Again, it was always the mothers fault for not doing so… But he always had time for a drink, going out partying or gigs, dates with girls and the money to be covered in crappy Batman tattoos, hence his nickname!

Moving out of the Tiddlers apartments was a huge relief for Sherlock as he had been living in a flat the size of a shoe box above a crack den with neighbours that can only be described as colourful for a little over a year. Moving into a new house share was something he was super excited for but had stupidly brought BatBoy & Whiney Penguin with him from the previous hell hole. Now we can't tell this story without mentioning the other villain...

Whiney Penguin is another person Sherlock considered a friend at one time from the Tiddlers flats and though he didn't move in with them, he was ALWAYS at the house. At first it wasn't a problem but later it was like have a couch troll who drank too much beer and didn't pay rent causing unnecessary problems in the house…

Whiney Penguin was a hard worker but would always be whining about something, normally why he wasn't successful in life one way or another… He would also always be dishing out life advice to people about things he was clueless about and even more so when on the smoke or drink.

Sherlock felt for him as he was also a victim of BatBoy, made to be one of his pawns and BatBoy tried to swooping a girl Whiney Penguin was trying to date at his workplace! Not only did he let BatBoy get away with this but further got rinsed for his money come payday for booze, food, tobacco etc. and of course whine to Sherlock about it later… Sherlock felt bad for him but at same time Whiney Penguin was the kind of guy who got fired for drinking at the bar every night he worked at, taking free booze for himself, all whilst he was on sick pay/leave and couldn't figure out why the bar let him go.

He wouldn't help himself is what we are trying to say here. He turned out to be a rotten individual and could not be happier to see back of him when Batboy started playing games with the rest of the housemates and turned Whiney Penguin into pawn for his manipulation tactics but more about that later... Let us tell you about the first day Sherlock moved into the house and introduce the heroes of this story…

Chapter 2: Sherlock & BatBoy move in, meeting the heroes of the house and they Sherlocks alarm clock almost got him in trouble!

When Sherlock moved out of the crazy flat into a much nicer house share with some of the loveliest people he had met, he had done so with Batboy… They had moved into a house share of 5, split 3 boys and 2 girls in total… You can already see the problems the villain is going to cause from his previous description.

When they first moved in Sherlock started getting close to one of the girls pretty quick and they began dating. We will call Queen Usmevbuk! An amazing girl, great personality, awesome smile and loved reading. They had a spark between them and got on really well from day one. She also had a great sense & timing for reminding Sherlock when to switch off from work especially when he was over doing things. He will always be grateful for their time together, they are still on good terms and consider a great friend to this day.

Sherlock also got to meet another lady, big sis Nuncatuve, she was just awesome! The BIG sister (don't want to make his little sister jealous now) Sherlock wish he had growing up. She gave Sherlock some amazing advice during their time as housemates. Even when she was blunt with him, especially when he got on her nerves. She would always tell him what he needed to hear when he needed to hear it, whether he liked it or not. Sherlock loved her for this and regrets not being in the house for farewell drinks when she moved back home…

When Sherlock and BatBoy moved in it was great and they were really lucky! Everyone in the house seemed amazing, super friendly and despite Sherlock waking the entire house up by accidentally plugging in his alarm clock with it set without realising. It would later go off at midnight on his first night at the house. The worse part is Sherlock and BatBoy had gone out for a drink to celebrate their escape from Tiddler and took them 20-30 minutes to get home to turn it off. To this day Sherlock appreciates that none of his new house mates drop kicked him in the head, which would have been completely understandable at the time and happily accepted after the madness he had lived through with Tiddler.

These two ladies were two of the best house mates Sherlock had after graduating from to secret spy academy (university) and know they are both living a happier life now without these two dumbasses around!

Chapter 3: Batboy tries swooping Queen Usmevbuk he gets rejected & tells Sherlock she had tried walking into his room with cookies...

Shortly after they moved in and Sherlock had apologised to his new housemates for leaving the alarm clock on after it went off whilst out for a celebration drink with Batboy and waking everyone up the night before. Luckily everyone was beyond cool with his mistake and the first couple months were great. No drama, Sherlock and Usmevbuk were having a great time getting to know each other but there was a point they hit a little hiccup. Sherlock confessed he wasn't ready for a serious relationship to Usmevbuk and they ended up having a couple of days they probably didn't talk to each other as much as normal. They sorted it in the end and continued dating until she moved back overseas to start new job.

However, there was a moment in those 2-3 days, a story BatBoy told Sherlock about Usmevbuk… BatBoy said she had tried to walk into his room uninvited with a plate of cookies, wanting to talk to him and that he had to ask her very politely to leave. Making himself out to be the hero of course… He tried to convince Sherlock how weird the situation was and bit of a bizarre conversations between, BatBoy, Sherlock and Whiney Penguin at the time. Sherlock brushed it off for whatever reason and it wasn't until later Sherlock realised what had actually happened…

Sherlock believed this little story of BatBoy until about a year last when Usmevbuk showed Sherlock the messages between herself & BatBoy slating Sherlock, telling her things about him that were completely untrue and just being a creep trying to get into her bedroom… BatBoy straight up tried swooping her from Sherlock, like an eagle hunting for prey and is something Sherlock later watched BatBoy do to the Whiney Penguin… (he later whined to Sherlock about this)

Luckily for Sherlock, Usmevbuk either had much better taste in men or could see through the mask he was putting on a lot sooner than Sherlock could! Quite possibly both as she was a smart girl. Why are we sharing this?

When BatBoy told Sherlock this story he wasn't really sure what to believe and remember putting it down to a culture difference as she was living away from her native country and thought it was completely harmless. Despite BatBoy trying to make it out to be something else and even though Sherlock didn't believe BatBoys take he had created another excuse that allowed the Bats plans go unseen for months!

The reason we are mentioning this is because even though Sherlock saw the signs of this villain, he still let him in!! Which is why we say to people seeing the villains is often not enough…

Chapter 4: Batboy tells Sherlock & Whiney Penguin the story of how Nuncatuve had tried to make a move on him & how he had to reject her because she was vulnerable...

So months go by and everything is OK in the house (at least on Sherlocks end). There was an evening Sherlock came home from work and saw BatBoy and the Whiney Penguin sat in the living room with a couple of beers chatting away. At this point they are all on friendly terms so he say hello as he would normally do to the villains.

Shortly after the greetings BatBoy jumps out of his seat and goes "Sherlock, you're never going to believe this... Nuncatuve tried to come on to me last night, it was really weird with everything going on and I had to make sure she was OK whilst letting her down in the nicest way... Don't tell her I told you though, as she might be embarrassed..."

This was when Sherlock started to slowly clock on to BatBoys mind games in the house as he knew Nuncatuve, one of the most awesome ladies he had ever met, wiser than a lot of people gave her credit for & just was completely out of character for her... Sherlock remembers brushing off the comment knowing it was BS but never spoke to Nuncatuve about this. She was going through some things at the time and it was just something that he would have no idea how to bring up even if he wanted to... This is where one of Sherlocks biggest regrets happened...

It was later revealed it had actually been BatBoy who had tried to take advantage of Nuncatuve who was going through a vulnerable time in her life and sometimes Sherlock wished he had slapped BatBoy harder. When BatBoys lies were eventually exposed Sherlock had to have a chat with Nuncatuve, she had some questions that he completely understood and was more than happy to provide answers for as Batboy had blurred so many realities as this point it was insane and everyone wanted the air clearing in the house. Sherlock remembers explaining to her that he had never believed she made a move on BatBoy, that he had been saying the same to everyone and was an exhausting 5-10 minute chat. Not because of Nuncatuve, as always she was a rockstar but because he was saying the exact same things that he was repeatedly telling to the Whiney Penguin about this situation. Who was stupid enough to believe BatBoys lies despite having evidence in screen shotted messages and much more…

Sherlock and the girls were all exhausted at this point from the energy the villains was leaching off everyone at the same time and was so happy everything was out in the open as things got so much better between Sherlock and the girls after this! There was one argument in the house that got Whiney Penguin banished from the house we will talk about in the next chapter…

Chapter 5: Batboy makes Whiney Penguin a pawn believing all his lies, the email they sent to letting agent lady to try and get Usmevbuk kicked out & Sherlock finally comes to his senses banning the Whiney Penguin from the house!

It was about a year or two into the tenancy things were really crazy. Batboys lies were starting to unravel between the girls and he was trying his absolute best to make Sherlock one of his pawns, which he was having none of!

At this point BatBoy had been slapped (next chapter) and was trying for dear life to gain back some kind of control of anything after his BS world was shattering around him... Him and the Whiney Penguin were also causing no end of trouble in the house, drinking every night, being noisy/disrespectful and it was causing lots of issues between everyone living together. It got to a point where you wasn't sure what was ok to talk about and what wasn't...

There was an evening where there was a huge fight in the house and Usmevbuk completely lost it on the villains (and rightfully so!) and they decided to retaliate. BatBoy & Whiney Penguin came down from BatBoys room one evening when Sherlock had just got home from performing in the bars of Cotham that night and immediately kicked off. Both of them tried to tell Sherlock how he needed to decide between boys or the girl as they spewed a variety of BS reasoning that BatBoy was trying to force Sherlock to believe...

They also decided to tell Sherlock their master plan to get Usmevbuk kicked out. Whiney Penguins exact words were, "If she thinks she will be living here much longer…" Not sure what or why he was whining to letting agent he didn't even live in the house! Anyway they had gone & sent an email to the letting agent lady, saying some disgusting things about Usmevbuk which were untrue that we will not repeat and basically trying to get her kicked out the house! Hilarious for Sherlock as he had so much ammunition against pair of them…

He knew they didn't have a leg to stand on and Sherlock reassured Usmevbuk this was the case. The letting agent lady called Sherlock shortly after this conversation with the creeps where he and the other house mates proceeded to expose BatBoy and what was really going on with him & Whiney Penguin! Their master plan to get her kicked out had backfired, BatBoy also had been rude/disrespectful to one of the loveliest ladies he had as a letting agent and was pretty sure he was already in his rent arrears...

It was made clear to BatBoy he wasn't to invite the Whiney Penguin back into the house, he was to no longer drink in the living areas and almost banished to his room like a small child after his disgusting behaviour... There was also another situation where Whiney Penguin was convinced Sherlock had written a message for UsmevBuk to send to Whiney Penguin based off the style of writing in a message she had sent him(mental we know!).

Sherlock was at a wedding gig at the time and Whiney Penguin was hounding his phone knowing he was at work. Usmevbuk warned me him he was on one so Sherlock decided not to deal with him until after the wedding when he got home later as he knew Whiney Penguin would be there. It is quite possible this is the same time when they sent the email to land lady but there was so much BS with dumb & dumber its hard to keep track what happened when on the timeline... But this is when Sherlock gave Whiney Penguin the ultimatum Bond or the Bat? (Please pick the bleeping Bat) Sherlock didn't care at this stage as he saw him for what he was but this was his last chance… He chose the Bat which Sherlock was beyond happy about to this day as quite frankly he was nothing but a little, fat, stupid, WHINEY PENGUIN!

BatBoy had to quickly move out after all of this and just shows how quick these villains lose their confidence & disappear the moment you EXPOSE their evil actions/plans to the world! This is the best way to repel these creatures who sadly walk among us... OK, the chapter you all been waiting for THE SLAP!

Chapter 6: What happened when Sherlock found out BatBoy tried swooping Usmevbuk, how BatBoy ended up kicking himself out of the house and using BatBoys dumb weakness against him!

So this is part of the story we are a little ashamed of because violence should only be a last resort and we hate to say, Sherlock wanted become DC's Joker at this point and kill the BatBoy! This was the day Usmevbuk showed him the messages on her phone between her & BatBoy. This is from when he tried swooping her during their 2-3 days of being off shall we say… This is also nearly a full year after the incident and revealed BatBoy had only been pretending to be Sherlocks friend the entire time for nearly 3 years!

Sherlock was angry, upset and borderline raging... He had helped this guy in so many ways, found the house for him, helped him with the same dodgy landlord Mr Tiddler, money, advice and just felt like an absolute fool for not seeing his BS sooner! To top things off BatBoy had decided to start stealing Sherlocks laundry tablets/powder the for a few weeks and had noticed this thievery from BatBoy! This will be important later...

BatBoy had been telling Sherlock from day one he considered him a real friend but was actually trying to play games with him. This was proof/wake up call Sherlock needed to begin exterminating the BatBoy! Don't mess with your friend if he's Joker as they will always have last laugh, especially if they are someone who is litcrally paid to destroy lives for a living!

So what did Sherlock do? Two things happened, first BatBoy came home with the Whiney Penguin later that evening, Sherlock was fully ready to turn into a Power Ranger and destroy the BatBoy... Sherlock took the first opportunity to bring it up, soon as that slimy snake slithered from the front door to the sofa and saw Sherlock glaring at him like the prey he was about to become... He spoke up and asked me "Whats with ya attitude Sherlock!?" Ooooo that was the kind of cocky comment Sherlock needed to set him off...

In front of Whiney Penguin, who had also had a girl swooped from BatBoy at this point remember he did nothing about this and is will be key later. Sherlock proceeded to call BatBoy out on all his BS in front of his friend and the pair of them sat there the entire time and did NOTHING! By time Sherlock was through with BatBoy he knew that things were about to change in the house… When Sherlock was done guess what Batboy did? Yep, he tried denying everything! Sherlock had seen the damn messages between him & Usmevbuk, BatBoys body language was beyond fidgety and his voice had gone up an octave when Sherlock mentioned the swooping! So to start denying it all just made Sherlock snap… It was morphing time!

That is when it happened, Sherlock had morphed into white Will Smith walked up & stood over a grown man covered in crappy batman tattoos whilst sat on a couch and… SLAP! The contact between the face & palm was beautiful and made an awesome snapping noise. If any of you have seen the newest

Power Rangers re-make the moment the red ranger slaps the bully in detention, that is what this was moment was like, YouTube it. BatBoys reaction was to have little struggle hug with Sherlock and ended up getting bullied to the floor by Sherlock. This isn't something he is proud of but it needed to be done in this situation because BatBoy thought he could take Sherlock on... He couldn't and Sherlock knew this, he wasn't a power ranger but knew enough MMA to snap the twig BatBoy was.

BatBoy also thought the Whiney Penguin would come to his rescue if Sherlock attacked him verbally or physically... Which also didn't happen, which was no surprise to Sherlock as quite frankly he was a little boy too. He had shown this to Sherlock when BatBoy swooped the girl from his workplace Whiney Penguin liked right in front of him, Sherlock & the entire house on a night out. He did nothing about it at the time but your guessed it whined about it to Sherlock later…

Batboy had been EXPOSED for the small child he was in front of everyone in his own house! Trust me when we tell you Sherlock fully felt like a power ranger at this point. After that conversation things completely changed for better, all of the normal housemates were now talking to each other, finding out about all of BatBoys lies and like any narcissist/villain he shrunk up, lost his confidence & stayed in his room for best of 2 weeks before leaving. The best way to get rid of villains is to use their own tactics against them and exposing them to the world is their biggest fear!

The second thing Sherlock did that he is a little more ashamed of but hilarious. Is how he got my revenge on BatBoy for stealing his laundry powder/tablets... BatBoy had a weakness & its was the most stupid weakness for a villain... His weakness was MINT! Yep, that's right, BatBoy was allergic to mint and would regularly go out drinking cocktails and eating chocolate with mint in them, setting off his allergies whilst scratching his skin and turning tomato red... Sherlock would normally feel bad for such a person but when you work as a bartender and proceed to buy drinks that you know has something you are allergic too in it. Sorry but you are a grade-A muppet and we lose all sympathy for you…

Anyway to cut a long story short, Sherlock decided his laundry wasn't smelling MINTY fresh enough that week and added concentrate mint marinade powder to his own laundry powder/tablets. You know, just to make sure my next loads were super MINTY fresh. He tried so hard not to laugh every time he saw that tool scratching like a chimpanzee the last couple weeks BatBoy was with living in the house. Sherlock even watched him one afternoon slyly stealing powder and then pretended he didn't notice! *We are crying writing laughing writing this

Chapter 7: Sherlock regretting not seeing the signs earlier, the amount of BS everyone in the house had to go through and the REASON Sherlock took anti-villain training in my spy programme

This time in Sherlocks life where he allowed BatBoy & Whiney Penguin linger caused so many issues for himself personally and was one of the happiest days of his life telling both of these individuals to do one!

But the thing that annoys Sherlock and regrets the most is not seeing and doing something about these villains sooner. Sherlock believes there were other housemates who probably had it a lot harder than him dealing with these two... Especially the girls in the house, Sherlock knew BatBoy was vile towards women and the thing he regrets the most is bringing these two dipshits into their lives… If he hadn't had brought them from the previous flat their lives would have been a lot easier and happier for the years he lived with them. We just hope the they are living a much happier life with no villains, lots of books and celebrating life to the fullest.

But with that regret came a transformation as Sherlock started taking training within personality/behaviour profiling, negotiation and dealing with narcissists/psychopaths from people in high risk interviewing/interrogation fields (army, CIA, FBI, police etc.) to make sure he never allows any VILLAINS like that into his life and near his close circle ever again!

Sherlock does business with Cothams Two-Chin whilst performing magic, mind-reading & picking pockets in his bar!

Chapter 1: The pain and internal confusion this villain caused Sherlock and how an amazing business relationship went up in flames!

This story takes place Cotham during the same period Sherlock was living with BatBoy & the Whiney Penguin. During this time everyone in the house was getting along, Sherlock had literally just moved into the new house at this time, had just left the Tiddler block of flats so when he started performing in this bar he was already been under a lot of stress at the time.

This was the first time Sherlock got fully rinsed in business by a villain and something that absolutely SHATTERED his confidence as a businessman & person 2-3 years after the event. He had given this villain so much of his time & energy that by the end of what was an amazing business relationship this villain completely blind-sided Sherlock out of nowhere. He flipped his coin and it was destiny Sherlock would get burned by them in the end…

Sherlock knew full well he had undersold his services to the bar, he didn't feel appreciated in what he was bringing to the business and despite the 5-star feedback from their clients! He still went above & beyond to help this villain anyway he could, special treatment for VIP guests & his family they needed and was shattered that someone who he looked up to, someone who he had taken so much advice from and also someone who at one point would have considered a friend turned on Sherlock in the way they did!

This is the story of when Sherlock was performing a residency magic weekly at a bar in Cotham and the general manager of the bar was none other than Cothams Two-Chin! Sherlock worked for Two-Chin for a couple years and when things were good, they were great, but that all changed when Two-Chin kept delaying payments for work Sherlock had already done and Two-Chins reasons kept changing to how/when Sherlock would be paid!

Sherlock ultimately walked away from the bar in Cotham but not before Two-Chin had destroyed his confidence AND making Sherlock out to be the villain to everyone he had spent years working with in Cotham... After this situation Sherlock went to search for the Batman to help him understand why people behave like this and a series of emails Two-Chin helped nudge his obsession of profiling and behaviour analysis to a new level (more on this in a later chapter). This is where Sherlock really got his teeth stuck into some life changing training in behaviour profiling and negotiation from some of the leading experts in the world!

Like all of these stories we have changed all names of characters to remain anonymous. This is one of the stories Sherlock wishes had a different ending and would definitely handle differently if he could go back as he was immature in his career and made some huge mistakes which we will point out in this story.

Chapter 2: First time Sherlock walks into the bar in Cotham, how relationship with Two-Chin started & meeting one the heroes, Grim Robin!

So before we continue just a little side note. Two-Face is one of our favourite villains in the Batman comics and as he always had an awesome 2 tone suit this general manager also had a great taste in suits. Despite not speaking to Two-Chin besides a brief meeting after parting ways in business. Sherlock has forgiven Two-Chin and wishes him nothing but the best for this & his family. In the fear of being sued by DC we have slightly changed the characters name from Two-Face to Two-Chin for minor comedy purposes as Two-Chin was actually in pretty good shape in real life. Sadly for him the name has a ring to it and is sticking. But before we continue let us rewind to first time Sherlock walked into that bar in Cotham!

So as some of you know Sherlock had a brief period of sofa-surfing between the years of 2014-2015 and it would have been sometime around this time he walked into the bar in

Cotham! He had just returned from his 2nd season at Island Lake Summer Camp teaching magic as a bunk counsellor and had decided to pursue his passion performing magic after briefly taking a my final "real job" as a charity fundraiser which lasted a whole 6 days!

Sherlock decided to try his luck in all the bars, restaurants and clubs which he had spent a good 6 months busking in between his first and second year at summer camp when he was fully sofa-surfing. Friends he trusted that would lend their sofa to Sherlock whenever possible. He will always be grateful for all the people put him up from a few days to weeks and some a couple of months. Sherlock wouldn't have been able to get the experience needed to be where he is today without you.

When Sherlock walked into Two-Chin's bar for the first time, Two-Chin wasn't even working there during this period as it was under different management. The first person who gave Sherlock a chance at that time was the assistant manager of the bar, whose codename for this story will be Grim Robin.

An amazing gent/manager, one of the nicest people Sherlock has had the pleasure of working with and has always supported Sherlocks business ventures at his lowest points... For this we will always be grateful to Grim Robin who we have only called this because he was on the wrong side of the heroes vs. villains for this story. So if there was ever a universe where Robin is good in batman but on the bad guys side, it's Grim Robin. Grim Robin was amazing at his job, always helped make things with Sherlock performing go smoothly & was eventually promoted in his industry! We hope he is enjoying a happy life to the fullest with his family nowadays!

Grim Robin introduced Sherlock to the general manager at the time and Sherlock is convinced to this day Grim Robin is a huge reason Sherlock went from busking in the bar for tips to eventually being paid 3 figures for one day a week to perform at the venue! This was perfect as these 2-3 years gave Sherlock the confidence to go up to ANYONE and start up a conversation! It also helped him perfect his craft as a performing magician, mind-reader & pickpocket plus it allowed him to pay his bills! He had hit the jackpot in so many ways, a few months later the general manager moved on to another venue which is when Sherlock would meet Two-Chin...

Two-Chin seemed like a nice guy, a big footie fan and had some great plans for bar which Sherlock was told was underperforming at the time. Sherlock introduced himself when Two-Chin started and they immediately got along fantastically. There were no red flags and Sherlock continued working in the bar as normal and was happy for many months. The time he was there between 2015-2018 was amazing right up until Two-Chin had screwed up payments of suppliers just after Christmas and it was everyone else's fault around him.

Sherlock later heard a rumour he was in trouble with his bosses at the same... Whether this is true or not, we don't actually know and past the point of caring really... Sadly Sherlock was one of many of his VICTIMS in line!

Chapter 3: Grim Robin leaves Cotham, associates start telling Sherlock stories about Two-Chin & one of Sherlocks biggest mistakes in this mission...

So we often say with villains you will get a "WTF" moment where they turn your life upside down and that completely throws you off emotionally. That moment can also come at any time... Days, weeks, months or in this case with Two-Chin ,YEARS... Sherlock didn't have any problems at all with Two-Chin during his time at the bar in fact, Sherlock was under the impression everything was amazing! He was constantly told about positive feedback from customers, managers would be bragging about smashing targets and everyone appreciated the service Sherlock was providing for the venue. He loved working with everyone and the customers were awesome!

Time went by and Sherlock would see staff come & go, customers would be having a good time at the weekend but slowly he would start hearing stories/rumours from other people about Two-Chin from his own associates.

Nothing major but things that looking back at Sherlock should have noted as a red flags to keep an eye on Two-Chin's behaviour...

The person Sherlock was saddest to see go was Grim Robin as he had been offered a promotion at another bar and despite being super happy that he was progressing in his career we can't deny being a little sad seeing him go… We are mentioning this part of the story because in the story you are going to understand why Sherlock left the bar, and more importantly, why he was so angry and hurt at the time! There was a bunch of other things going on in Sherlocks life during this time, had been living in the flat above the crack den and had only just moved into his new house share!

But it doesn't excuse what Sherlock did when Two-Chin started playing his manipulation games with him and that was Sherlock started bad mouthing Two-Chin to other people behind is back. Something he is not proud of and know full well he had bumped into Grim Robin after he had left whilst Sherlock was in his final weeks working at the bar and had told Grim Robin exactly what he thought about Two-Chin during this very emotional time for him...

We want to be clear here, he wasn't just exposing Two-Chin like he should have... He had turned into Cotham's Joker & wanted blood... He was overstepping the mark, making accusations with no solid proof, saying things that were totally unprofessional and if we could go back and take them back we would. But we learn from these mistakes and move forward in our life.

Chapter 4: Two Chin is late paying Sherlock,the BS reasoning Two-Chin gave and how he made Sherlock out to be a bad guy!

So fast forward to Christmas 2017 and things at the Cotham bar are buzzing! They are the busiest Sherlock has ever seen the venue every weekend, the energy between Sherlock and DJ's was amazing (shout out to DJ's for providing serious tunes whilst performing close up magic in Gotham) and the feedback from ALL the managers & customers is amazing!

We get to one of the last days of Christmas & Sherlock is upstairs packing up his stuff (throwing cards in his bag before going home). Two-Chin comes out the office screaming and full on WWE choke-slams a chair in the restaurant, he picked it up and launched it! We don't know what exactly happened in that office that day to make him do this but we can make an educated guess. But Sherlock had NEVER seen him like this, Two-Chin was normally calm, cool and collective... Nothing about this was in his character, he had turned into the Incredible Hulks little boy throwing chairs around the bar/restaurant like small green child. Similar to when someone has just taken toys away from a child and they start a tantrum but it wasn't anything to do with Sherlock so he headed home...

Now when working at Two-Chin's bar they would always pay Sherlock 3 weeks in arrears meaning he does a day of performing magic and then he would get paid 3 weeks later! This had always been the case, bar maybe 2-3 occasions where Two-Chin said he would have to pay me in cash from the venue safe... It rarely happened and when it did Sherlock would have to wait maybe an extra week the most to get it sorted...

However this time it would be different. Just after Christmas Two-Chin had "forgotten", got a "non-obligational order" from head office or whatever BS reasons he would give that Sherlocks payments would have be delayed 3 weeks... This happened another 2 times meaning Sherlock was waiting for payment 9 weeks after doing jobs and not being paid and to top things off Two-Chin had decided to cancel dates he had agreed to book ONE day before the events happening! He tried pulling this stunt at least 3 times despite agreeing a 7-day notice cancellation policy...

These last minute cancellations had cost Sherlock gigs & money he had turned down because he had made a commitment to the bar (despite them withholding payment due to non-obligation things from head office or whatever BS excuse Two-Chin gave) and because he was away from the bar due to being in hospital Sherlock rarely saw him at the venue during this time. He wouldn't pick up his phone and rarely respond to emails especially with invoices attached like he normally would...

During this time Sherlock just felt like Two-Chin was taking him for a fool and he was! Sherlock started noticing he was getting angry throughout the week and wasn't enjoying performing at the bar anymore. He wanted to move on and decided to send a bold email which worked (kind of).

This whole situation is exactly why Sherlock does business the way he does now with signed agreements and getting payment BEFORE the events! You don't get Amazon to send you your shopping and then pay for it do you?

What makes the whole story even more hurtful for Sherlock is he would visit venues of the company from the bar and the bar itself after parting ways in business with Two-Chin. For the first few months every single person Sherlock bumped into who he had worked with during this time at the bar had all been told by Two-Chin Sherlock had acted unprofessional during his time at the bar which was just unbelievable as you will find out in the following chapters...

Chapter 5: The moment that changed everything in Sherlocks career and how a series of emails between Sherlock and Two-Chin set him on a path to train with the Batman to battle with villains in future!

So after months of payments being delayed, being messed around by managers and quite frankly spoken down to after an amazing Christmas period, Sherlock had enough! He wanted to stop performing at the bar in Cotham but he was too scared of offending anyone & was still attached to all the amazing memories with the staff & customers.

Sherlock decided after multiple failed attempts calling Two-Chin it was time to send an email explaining how he felt under-appreciated recently, that last minute cancellations had cost him a lot of money as he had turned down better paid work committing to dates requested by Two-Chin and that he was changing his prices from 2-3 weeks time (raising them from £150 to £200 per week). Sherlock also said he will now be needing a contract signed in future to ensured that he gets paid on time! A standard business practice that EVERYONE business does! The email ended:

"I absolutely love working with you guys, customers are always fun, staff and managers are amazing and that is why I do everything in my power to provide the best entertainment/ networking services for your customers and business at the best price possible. But I have felt massively under appreciated due to how these cancellations have been handled recently. I understand the situation with head office and lockdown period but I cannot overlook cancellations with such short notice. I hope we can continue working together in the future and I look forward to hearing back from you. P.S. I hope the knee is all well and good."

The response Sherlock got from Two-Chin shook him... He didn't think his email was confrontational, he thought there was a possibility of him keeping the residency but it was very slim and thought that Two-Chin would understand. Sherlock thought they had a good relationship but it turns out he was just a number to Two-Chin, a cost and someone he was willing to throw under the bus and make sure it would be difficult for Sherlock to work within the venue or the company again...

Chapter 6: Two-Chin's responses to Sherlocks email, his first time directly manipulating Sherlock and how it damaged him for 2-3 years after this mission...

We know we left you on a cliffhanger in the last chapter but this series of emails was something that inspired Sherlock to look deeper into the content analysis side of profiling, reading peoples emotions through written communication like messages, social media posts and EMAILS! So when Sherlock found his mentors, every single one of them went through these emails with him and analysed between the lines!

We are sharing the emails & the lessons Sherlocks secret spy mentors shared with him on his training courses so you can spot these signs yourself in the future and nip them in the butt before they become a problem or throw you off your emotions like Two-Chin did to Sherlock! We have only shared key parts of the emails with the most valuable lessons and made sure everyone remains anonymous. It is the lessons within these emails we want to focus on. So let's get into it this was Two-Chins response:

"I understand your frustration but you have to understand from a business perspective that P+L and bottom line profit are king."

-Amazing is started well & we are speaking same language.

"That being said I also do not appreciate being dictated to on price and terms and conditions. Backing a company/ business, especially with an experienced manager, into a corner dictating price is the wrong way to conduct business, I feel £150 per day is a FAIR price and can confirm without further discussion that I am not willing to pay any more."

- This is Two-Chin's first bit of manipulation, his use of the word FAIR! Subtly insinuating Sherlock must stupid/ignorant to the proposition. He was, he was being extremely underpaid & being mistreated at the time for what he brought to the table. Ask anyone who worked with him or saw Sherlock perform at Two-Chin's bar performing!

-Take note of his language here "especially with an experienced manager…" Sherlock had never questioned or brought up his experience as manager so why is he bringing it up now?

- Also take note of him being not like being dictated by price, terms & conditions and what Sherlock is doing is "bad practice" in business however in the next part he does the EXACT same thing! The difference is he talks about things completely unrelated to the negotiation to throw Sherlock off... And it worked!

- It is also worth noting keeping your promises like paying suppliers on time & given more than 24 hours notice cancellation when you agreed 7 days is also a "good practice" in business. This makes sure you avoid being dictated by priced, terms & conditions by any business owners as you will find we can do whatever the &^%$ we want!

"Your residency in Cotham currently equates to £8k p/a outside of the extras we book in during Xmas and New Year. The extra £2.5k you are proposing will pay for my staff parties throughout the year amp host other Live entertainment."

-Another red flag! WTF is all this waffle about the extra £2.5k will host staff parties throughout the year and host other live entertainment. More fluff to throw Sherlocks emotions and nothing to do with the actual problem Two-Chin had caused!

"If you are confident that you can earn more than this elsewhere (as a business man) I would understand your decision to look at alternative opinions."

- This last line had Sherlock questioning his decisions (especially as a businessman) for YEARS and was not necessary from Two-Chin at all! Especially since he knew Sherlocks circumstances at the time, if Two-Chin had done is job as a manager by giving Sherlock more than 24 hours notice for cancellations and not make him wait 9 weeks for payment ignoring his calls/emails they wouldn't be having this conversation in the first place. But it can't be the villains fault as they can never look bad to the outside world...

So what happened after this well Sherlock went straight back into victim-identity mode we will explain the next chapter...

Chapter 7: Sherlocks regrets with bad mouthing Two-Chin behind his back, not listening to other people around him and allowing Two-Chins manipulation to affect him years due to no forgiveness!

So what was Sherlocks actual response to Two-Chin's emails at the time... Well he just went straight back into that victim-identity mentality and made danced like Two-Chins little puppet. Sherlocks response probably did more to hurt the relationship & he never got a response to this email. They decided a week later, either in a meeting or phone call, to part ways in business. As like we said Sherlock no longer had the same feeling and joy of working there due to what had happened with Two-Chin and this particular series of emails! And we are pretty sure Two-Chin was pissed off with Sherlock at this point too. Sherlock sent him the following email word for word just so you understand how this threw him emotionally and how much he care about the relationship between him and Two-Chin:

"Thanks for a speedy response. I apologise if the email came across that way as that was not my intention. I struggle to communicate these kind of things in writing and frustration of recent events probably hasn't helped. That's not your fault and for this I am sorry. I have also miscalculated what you guys pay me per year (I went by figures from last year which I did not take into account lower fees you were paying earlier in the year) I was aiming to be paid 7.5-8k a year which is what is being paid now. So you are right £150 per day is fair and now wish I had gone about the previous email differently. If you would still be happy to have me on a weekly basis for £150 that would be fantastic and will get the contract over to you by tomorrow morning. Honestly, I was just upset of short notice given for today's cancellation as it has put me under a lot of pressure being my slowest period of year and recently moving house. I just needed to tell someone at company and probably worded it the wrong way. I hope this doesn't effect the relationship we have and I do appreciate you reaching out to the other venues on my behalf. I hope to hear from you soon and look forward to seeing you back in Cotham"

We're not going to go through this email in detail but you can clearly see Sherlock had fallen for his trap, apologising for nothing he had caused and how hurt he was looking back! So why are we sharing this story & specifically the emails? Well the language in these emails were completely different from anything Sherlock had received from Two-Chin before and remember feeling so confused and hurt by this when Two-Chin had manipulated Sherlock to take late payments so he could "manage" bar. You know what crooks are like in Cotham and language patterns is something Sherlock actively listens out for in ALL his interactions, spoken or written today.

This was the moment Sherlock was inspired to really sink his teeth into the world of personality/behaviour profiling and negotiation to make sure if something like this ever happened again he would know what to do. In this particular case case with Two Chin Sherlock started off well and should have stuck to his guns in the email and replied, "no problem all the best in future and will finish up this weeks event or can cancel immediately…" Instead he ended up worrying that I was missing out on, which is funny looking back as he never worked with/for Two-Chin again and was probably one of the best decisions he made for his business! Sherlock worked maybe a couple more weeks at the bar after these emails and his last day in Gotham was fun!

Sherlocks last day at the bar was super fun, for some reason that spark he had before this madness had come back and it was like a weight had been lifted off his shoulders. All the customers were amazing that day he got to read minds, steal peoples items to give them back and was even having an amazing time with some new hypnosis he was working on with some of the regulars. It was honestly a great day but at the same time extremely weird one... We will be honest we don't ever remember saying goodbye to Two-Chin on that day, Sherlock would bump into him later with some civil greetings between them and wished him all the best but the on the day itself. Maybe a formal handshake and goodbye maybe we honestly couldn't tell you…

Saying goodbye to all the staff on the other hand was a little harder, as Sherlock had literally spent years getting to know some of the people and seen some of them go through multiple promotions! It was sad saying goodbye to his friend, the ground floor DJ! Not only had he provided him with some of the best jams to perform close-up magic in the bar but an awesome guy who helped Sherlock out massively with advice early in my business and super grateful for his wisdom in the underground days of his magic career.

Looking back at this situation there is a whole bunch of things Sherlock would have done different but as we said he was in a tough spot with other villains & personal circumstances, being a young businessman and his temper has always been his own worst enemy. We have already shared the regret of bad mouthing Two-Chin to others earlier and Sherlocks temper was a huge factor in this...

Sherlock was hurt, angry and confused at the time and not being able to control his temper with these emotions has always got him into trouble. It would be of no surprise to Sherlock if any of these comments made their way back to Two-Chins ears and did more damage to the relationship than anything else. Big reason why Sherlock makes a point to keep his temper and mouth under control years later.

Looking back we also wish Sherlock had listened to more people around his as there were flags he missed, stories he had heard and probably even ignored. But if one good thing came from this experience it was it inspired Sherlock to take action to make sure it never happens again! But his biggest regret from all of this without a shadow of a doubt the fact he has only been able to forgive the villain 1 maybe 2-3 years after the event (2021) when writing this story...

It was almost like Two-Chin's ghost was around constantly whispering in Sherlocks ear, "as a business man are you being fair?" making him constantly question his decisions in life/

business holding him back. The thought of Two-Chin often made Sherlock angry, upset and confused all over again. Reminding himself, "after everything he gave to you and the bar, after everything we had achieved together, WHY!?!?!" It felt like he straight up spit in Sherlocks face & kicked him in the nuts the way he had treated him at the end of their business relationship. It was probably worse since at one stage Sherlock considered Two-Chin a friend and actually someone he looked up as a professional/business man.

We are not sure what Two-Chin is doing now but hope him, his family are living a happy, healthy life and he is doing great at whatever it is he doing. Sherlock was growing as a businessman & as a person back when he was performing at Two-Chin's bar. He is beyond grateful for the experience and cherishes the memories he has there & will continue to grow without any manipulative people in his life, whether they are experienced or not!

Our number one tip for dealing with villains is ALWAYS avoid that victim-identity mentality as the villains can smell this from a mile off and in Sherlocks case he had shared far too much of his personal life with this villain. We have no doubt Two-Chin was using Sherlocks own victim mentality against him to get what he needed out of Sherlock looking back and Two-Chin discarded him like something on the end of shoe when no longer needed/wanted Sherlock... Don't give the villains anything they can use against you and remember to do you to the absolute fullest!

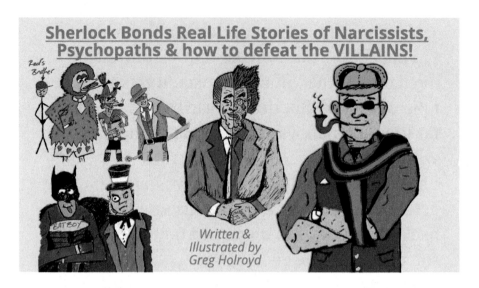

**Sherlock Bonds Real Life Stories of Narcissists, Psychopaths & how to defeat the VILLAINS!**

Written &
Illustrated by
Greg Holroyd

De-Brief Summary: Looking back at these missions and developing new spy weapons to repel future villains who walk among us...

So these are 3 mission debriefs is where Sherlock Bond had to deal with and sometimes defeat VILLAINS. We have tried to tell these stories in a funny way to highlight the important lessons between the lines (There are probably more but these are the key points we hope readers will take away from these hilarious stories).

1. Villains are insecure people who attack others to make themselves feel better for their own wrong doings. Avoiding the victim-identity mentality as they smell this from a mile away and it attracts them like flys to... Avoiding this is the best repellent whilst threatening them with abandonment or threatening to expose them to the world are weapons to exit these relationships!

2. Seeing the signs of the villains is often not enough... There are lots of signs that reading back we would have easily handled differently now but the biggest thing we would say is setting BOUNDARIES. Whether it was believing everything BatBoy said, allowing Two-Chin to book Sherlock with no agreement... We didn't set any boundaries in any of these relationships and allowed the villains run wild. Always set boundaries and if they are broken act on consequences!

3. The lesson that is hidden within the pages is the 5 step cycle every single villain will take

you through. Love-bombing/Courtship, Persuasion, Devaluation, Control and finally Discard... We talk about this more in Sherlock Bonds online courses, The Sherlock Bond Persuasive Negotiation System & Gregs talks but it is worth noting these cycles can be short, like with Two-Chin and the sudden "WTF" moment, or they can be longer like BatBoy & Tiddlers BS experiences...

Just by being aware of the cycle now allows us to see where people think we are in the cycle within our relationships with villains and allows us to set a plan to deal with any problems they may cause before they happen (we still have to deal with them from time to time but much better now). What is even more rewarding and empowering for ourselves is we can see when our friends and family are in these cycles to help give them the advice and the tools to repel, handle or exit these hairy relationships... It is a big reason why we love doing what we do as a speaker & coach at the MagicSpeaker!

If you read the book back you should be able to see exactly what stage of the cycle Sherlock was in moments of certain chapters of these stories and hopefully the lessons will help you avoid falling for the same traps as we did...

We want to say a huge thank you for reading these stories and really do hope you had as much fun reading as we did writing them! If we could ask you one favour...

Take a screen shot of the cover and write a post out on your social media page telling all your family & friends you had a blast reading this. Feel free to tag me in the post (Greg Holroyd not Sherlock Bond) and let me know which was your favourite story and if the book has helped you at all.

You will be glad to know we have only shared a portion of my story and depending on how this new part of our journey goes, as we have re-discovered a passion for writing short stories & sharing these with you, so who knows, Sherlock Bond may go back into the archives and share more crazy debriefs! So it is not goodbye for now as this is only the first edition of this book!